WILD WORK

WHO ROLLS THROUGH FIRE?

WORKING ON A MOVIE SET

Mary Meinking

www.raintreepublishers.co.uk
Visit our website to find out
more information about
Raintree books.

To order:
☎ Phone 0845 6044371
🖷 Fax +44 (0) 1865 312263
🖳 Email myorders@raintreepublishers.co.uk

Customers from outside the UK please telephone +44 1865 312262

Raintree is an imprint of Capstone Global Library Limited,
a company incorporated in England and Wales having its
registered office at 7 Pilgrim Street, London, EC4V 6LB –
Registered company number: 6695582

Text © Capstone Global Library Limited 2011
First published in hardback in 2011
The moral rights of the proprietor have been asserted.

Edited by David Andrews, Nancy Dickmann, and Rebecca
Rissman
Designed by Victoria Allen
Picture research by Liz Alexander
Leveled by Marla Conn, with Read-Ability.
Originated by Dot Gradations Ltd
Printed and bound in China by Leo Paper Products

ISBN 978 1 4062 1679 0 (hardback)
14 13 12 11 10
10 9 8 7 6 5 4 3 2 1

British Library Cataloguing in Publication Data
Meinking, Mary.
    Who rolls through fire? : working on a movie set. -- (Wild
work)
    1. Motion picture industry--Employees--Juvenile
literature.
    I. Title II. Series
    791.4'3'0293-dc22

Acknowledgements
The author and publisher are grateful to the following for
permission to reproduce copyright material: 2005 TopFoto
p. **19**; Alamy pp. **4** (© Melvyn Longhurst), **6** (© Photos 12), **7**
(© Jeff Morgan The Arts), **10** (© AWB Photography), **13** (©
imagebroker), **14** (© Mike Goldwater), **17** (© Jeff Mood), **18**
(© JHP Attractions), **20** (© LHB Photo), **21** (© Photos 12),
25 (© eddie linssen), **27** (© Adrian Sherratt); Corbis pp. **5** (©
Christophe d'Yvoire/Sygma), **9** (© Ann Johansson), **11** (©
Francois Duhamel / DREAMWORKS/Bureau L.A. Collection),
15 (© Luc Roux), **28** (© Luc Roux); Getty Images pp. **8** (Tom
Kingston/WireImage), **12** (Ian Wingfield), **24** (Doug Allan/
The Image Bank), **26** (Warrick Page); Press Association
Images p. **16** (Ted S. Warren/AP); Rex Features pp. **23**
(NBCUPHOTOBANK), **29** (© Magnolia/Everett); The Kobal
Collection p. **22** (Walt Disney Pictures/Walden Media).

Background design features reproduced with permission
of Shutterstock (© Jenny Horne).

Cover photograph reproduced with permission of Corbis
(© Yuri Kochetkov/epa).

Some words are shown in bold, **like this**. You can find
out what they mean by looking in the glossary.

Contents

Movie time

Lights, camera, action! Welcome to the movie set. It takes hundreds of people to make a film. Everyone has a job to do.

Some people act in front of the camera. Even more people work behind the **scenes** to make the film a success.

Action!

Directors are like storytellers. They turn the words in the **script**, or story, into a film. They plan each **scene** of the film.

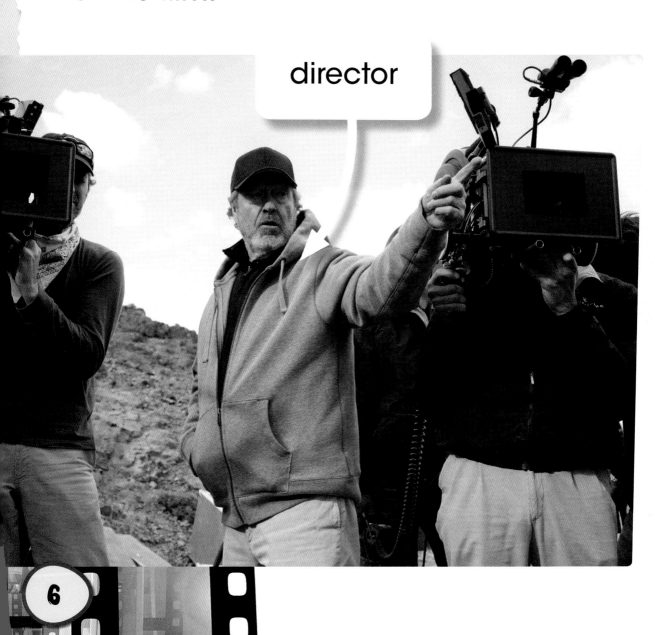

director

Directors tell the actors what they should be doing in front of the camera. They also direct the light, sound, and camera crews.

Fame and fortune

Actors need to do more than just remember to say their lines in front of a camera. They make believe they are the **characters** they're playing. Their voice, crooked smile, or limp makes their character seem more real.

DID YOU KNOW?

Famous film stars have their own trailers. They sleep, eat, or change there between **scenes**.

People go to places such as Hollywood, New York, or **Bollywood** in Mumbai, India to get into movies. Only a few become stars. Many become **extras** in group **scenes**.

extras

Some actors are children. They can
only act a few hours each day.
They have to keep going to school.
Teachers come to the film set to
help them with their homework.

Looking their best

Hair **stylists** style actors' hair. They make sure the actor's hair doesn't change from one **scene** to the next.

Makeup artists can add crooked noses, bloody cuts, or make actors look much older. Foam is **moulded** around actors to make them look like monsters, aliens, or animals.

Costume designers find or make the clothes used in films. The clothing must match the time and place of the film's story. Designers plan what every actor wears, from head to toe.

These actors are wearing the type of clothing worn in France during the 1500s.

What a stunt!

Stunt people take the place of some film stars for dangerous **scenes**. Stunt people know how to do the stunts safely.

Remember you're not
a stunt person, so don't
try any of these tricks!

Some stunt people are even set on fire.
They put on special clothes under their
costumes. They cover their costumes
with a liquid that burns without hurting
them. But it still can be dangerous!

17

Stunt people are used when **characters** are in fights or fall. They're needed when cars explode or tumble off a cliff.

DID YOU KNOW?

In a "stunt fight," stunt people stand a few steps apart. One person pretends to punch. The other pretends to get hit. The camera behind them can't see that it wasn't a real punch.

All set?

The art **department** finds everything that you see in a film, except for the actors and their costumes. They buy or make the **props** used in each scene. Model makers build tiny buildings, trees, and aeroplanes.

This model ship and city
look life-size on camera!

Computer magic

Computer images can show what people can't build. They can show thousands of soldiers, bugs, or space ships. Computers can make aliens and monsters look real.

Sometimes actors are filmed in front of a green screen. Then a dangerous place is filmed. The computer combines the two shots. It looks like the actors are in that dangerous place.

Roll film

Camera operators film the movie. There are several cameras filming at the same time. But they film from different places. One of them will get the perfect shot the **director** needs.

They film in all types of weather.
Sometimes they're underwater or
next to a speeding car.

Lights and sound

People called **gaffers** are in charge of lights. They shine **spotlights** or coloured lights on the scenes. Gaffers use huge white cards to bounce light into dark spots.

boom operator

Boom operators hold long-armed **microphones** over the actors. They capture every whisper, grunt, and sneeze. **Sound effects** are added to films to make them sound more real.

Could you work on a film set?

Everyone on the film crew must work long and hard. They must like travelling because they could have to film anywhere in the world.

The film crew must work together as
a team. Everyone wants the film to
be the next big hit!

Glossary

Bollywood the centre of India's film business

boom a microphone on a long pole

character person who an actor represents in a film or play

department group with its own jobs

director person who guides the actors and says how a film is made

extras background actors who don't speak in films

gaffer person who does the lighting on a film set

microphone a device that captures sound so it can be recorded

moulded fitted into a shape

props objects used in a film or play

scene part of a film that is set in one place

script a written play broken down with actors' parts

sound effects made-up sounds

spotlight a strong beam of light shone in one area

stunt a dangerous act done by someone

stylist person who cuts and shapes hair

Find out more

Books to read

Backstage at a Movie Set, Katherine Wessling (Rosen Book Works, 2003)

Break a Leg! The Kid's Guide to Acting and Stagecraft, Lise Friedman (Workman Publishing Company, 2002)

Stunt Man, Stephen Rickard (Ransom Publishing, 2010)

Websites to visit

http://www.stuntacademy.com/index.html
This website teaches young people how to be stunt people.

http://www.bafta.org/awards/childrens/
The British Academy of Film and Television Arts website has a section on award-winning children's films.

Index